boxed memories

poems

adela muhic

1st edition.
ISBN: 9781086414745

Cover Design: madebybodeine@gmail.com

Contact me:
Instagram - @4dela
Email - adelamuhic17@gmail.com

for anyone that needs it.
& when i needed it most,
thank you to whoever was there
/love is my parents, my brother, & my other half/

I shoved them in a box, crinkled up their edges and buried them deep
I do not want these memories anymore, please hide them from me I cried
I begged the boxes to never show their faces again, I couldn't handle it
All those tears, all that heartbreak, all that depression
You may not want them now, but you will need them later
For now they will stay your boxed memories, until you're ready to tell their stories

words are so powerful
despite you being far gone,
you will always live within these pages
that old version of me and the old version of you
will always be written down, tucked away…
and maybe someday, somebody will decide
our story is worth reading
-atleast i think it is-

we were so obsessed with growing up
we forgot to enjoy the time we had left with each
other
if we knew, maybe we could've changed our ending
maybe we could've made it last
maybe, we wouldn't have fallen *out* of love

i feel like i would give anything to go back
& maybe warn myself about a few things
how different would i be if i avoided you?

you got your feelings hurt and i didn't mean to do
that
but i can't go back and change what i did
-enjoy the taste of your own medicine-

i'm at war with myself and
i don't know when i should surrender
it feels as if i'm being suffocated
by my own two hands and
for some reason,
my grip keeps getting tighter and tighter
-wake up please-

i keep telling myself to wake up but it's not working
having conversations with myself
 & the old me keeps lurking
-does anybody hear my screams?-

there's so many people that
hold me to the highest standard
if only they knew what went on inside my head,
they'd reconsider
because even i wouldn't pick me if i had a choice
-it's kind of sad hearing that out loud-

i've been asked numerous times lately
why i'm so distant
i keep repeating the same line,
"my heart has been broken"
and i get asked the same question,
"which guy was stupid enough to do that to you?"
my same answer is,
"i was stupid enough to do it to myself"
-it's me. i broke my own heart. it happens-

and through it all…
i managed to defeat my demons
and i pray that you defeat yours too
-*good luck babe*-

for all of those struggling out there...
i know you think you're not enough
i know you're scared
of what's gonna happen to you
i know you're ready to give up,
but you will prevail.
you always do

inflicting pain on yourself
feels so good in the moment,
nothing else on your mind…
i wish i hadn't done it
it's not worth it

and when they ask me about you
and all the memories we created
i hope i don't forget too,
to include the times i waited
alone and in search of anybody
because it was really me you hated

it's so frustrating loving somebody that
doesn't want to do anything to change
for the better

but it's not up to you to nurture and baby him

it's not on *you*
that he isn't bettering *himself*

my dreams told me to chase you
my dreams told me we'd be so happy
my dreams told me everything will work out

my dreams lied to me
this nightmare of a reality is what i have
and you're not here
and i will be okay
i think

to any person no longer in my life:
good luck and please don't come back

you are the person i write about at 4am
when i'm aching and can't sleep
he's the person i write about at 4pm
when i'm beaming and can't contain it

as much as he is my sun
for some reason,
i hold onto parts of the moon
even when i don't want to

and as much as one person breaks you down
at the end of the day
it's still up to you to pick yourself up
and get through it

after you two break up for the first time
things will never be the same afterwards
new me + new you
don't go very well with each other
-no matter how much we try to force it-

you've transformed yourself into a new person
so don't fall back into your old habits
no matter how much
they keep calling you back to them

i know how it is to feel
helpless, useless, worthless
but these are just your demons
trying to get you to break
you will overcome them, it's only a matter of time
-i wish you could see your own strength-

i knew you weren't good for me
i knew i wasn't good for you
i knew that you knew this as well
yet, we still craved each other
in the morning, in the night
we didn't want to be together,
but we didn't want to let go
it was toxic...
-and i think a part of us knew that as well-

i would tell you to leave, but i'd block the door
i would say don't call me, but i'd end up calling you
i would want you to quit bothering me,
but i couldn't be without you
i never knew what I wanted, i'm sorry
i still don't know

there is so much heartbreak in the world
so just hold me a little tighter and a little longer
while i try to forget

it's pretty pathetic
the fact that
you have to threaten breaking up with him
for him to finally try to act right
pay attention to the signs
and get the hell out of there

if you're trying to get things to go back
to how they used to be,
you'll be stuck forever
-trust me, i know-

i can't imagine giving my all to one person anymore
none of you deserve that from me

i tried to cut off all my friends
before i completely lost myself
i didn't want to burden them with my issues
i didn't want anybody to share
the pain that i was feeling
i taught myself it'd be better to face this alone
and that's just how depression
makes sure to isolate you

it's like i changed into a different person
right in front of you
and you never noticed
or maybe you did notice
and just didn't care to say anything
-but i hope you just didn't notice & would still care-

quit giving yourself away so freely
to people that wouldn't even fight for you
-i hate seeing you go through that-

you deserve the best
and i'm sorry
these boys didn't know how to give it to you

i know that you are so tired, my love
it's okay to rest, please do
just promise me
you will never stop fighting
for what you deserve

you're just a girl who craves the simple things in life
a hand to hold and loving arms
to welcome you home
i wish more people knew that about you

i know some people might be intimidated by you
but you're just a girl
with a golden heart and pure intentions
i wish more people knew that about you, too

even though you might not see it
you are a better person than i am
you're forgiving, optimistic,
and always have love to give
everybody could learn a thing or two from you
/the girl who had too much love to give/
-her name is amra-

no matter how much wrong a person does to you,
you always put all the blame on yourself
you would never say these kinds of horrible things
to other people,
so why do you say it to yourself?

it pains me to see what you
allow others to do to you

i want you in the sunshine
i want you in the rain
i want you at your highs
i want you at your lows
i want whatever is going to be thrown at me
i just want you to be there, too

always be kind to yourself first,
at the end of the day you're all
that you have and you owe yourself
at least that much

i knew that once
i could look out into a thunderstorm
and not become engulfed in it,
i had achieved peace

i no longer felt controlled by the rain
because i knew i embodied the sunshine

i turned into a broken person that craved the pain
it was as if i had gotten so used to being hurt,
i felt comforted whenever it happened
how the hell did i get to this point?

i wish i could just hold you
and shield you from all that's going on
outside of these four walls
but i can't and it's killing me
-stay safe-

it's so hard for me to have small talk with people
when there's so many issues in the world
we need to talk about instead

i'm no longer pushing myself to be better for *you*
i'm pushing myself to be better for *me*
-character development-

that burden i once carried
that weighed heavy on my tired heart
is now gone
and I'm finally letting peace come in
and settle down in her new home
-*stay*

you deserve a crown full of flowers,
on a bright and warm day
the sun will greet you
as she recognizes your strength
you're beaming as bright as i am, she'll say to you
and you will let the wind hug you and you will know:
you are finally free

we believed that all the problems we had
were normal for relationships
we found comfort in the toxicity of it
& that's how we should've known
 it wasn't meant to be
-and it never will be-

i wrote you letters
& you didn't even want to read them
-wasted times-

nobody is going to love you
as much as you love yourself
so, give yourself the love story
you've been waiting for

i held it together
i held it down
you can never deny all i did for you

you stopped appearing in my dreams
you started appearing in my nightmares
-switched the flip-

anything that you can do for me,
i can do for myself
maybe that's why
i don't need you anymore

i'm so bad at goodbyes,
maybe that's why i just avoid them
maybe i just can't stand
the look in your eyes as i walk away
maybe my heart can't be put through
you convincing me to stay
maybe it's because i know
if i let you hold my hand one more time,
i'd stay
-i'm bad at goodbyes because i don't want to say goodbye-

almost everything that i've done
in the heat of the moment
i've ended up regretting
so please take a minute to breathe & think
before acting on anything
the person you'll end up hurting the most
is yourself

i'm pretty sure i loved you
i just never told you
would it have changed anything?
would you have stayed?
-i'll never know-

at some point i will have to let you go,
i'm well aware
she should have all of you,
not just bits and pieces
you cannot fully be with her
while you're still in love with me
but it's okay... choose *her,* go to *her*
i'm not the one for you, my love
-contradictions-

i'm undeniably in love
with the person you used to be
i'd give anything to find him
and spend a day with him…
old me + old you were unstoppable
/until the universe stopped us/

i no longer crave the thunderstorms
i now crave the sunshine
but i've learned to see the beauty
in the thunderstorm & to thank her
for giving me my sweet, sweet sunshine

promises were meant to be broken,
right?
at least with you they were

you painted me as the bad guy
and i hope your brush breaks in half
-fuck your painting-

you pointed the gun at me and
i was no longer afraid of you
pulling the trigger
you've already killed me a couple times

i've met Love a couple of times
& only really got to know her once
she came in unexpectedly
and shook me to my core
it's not that i wish i never met her,
i just thought she'd be better to me

you won't listen to anybody's advice
even though a part of you knows you're wrong
you will have to get hurt in order to learn

i don't know what you're going through,
but i hope you make it out to the other side

i spent months
trying to rebuild myself after you left
i needed that to realize how weak i was
and what pieces i needed to strengthen
-you're not welcome back-

you don't lose your value
just because someone else
doesn't know how to appreciate it
it's not your fault they don't know your love

i wanted peace
i wanted peace within myself so badly
i did whatever it took
and i ventured wherever i had to
just to restore what you robbed me of

the seat next to me is empty
the seat next to me is where
you should be
the plane is about to take off
& i'm sorry i couldn't wait for you
but i have to go and leave my worries
to fly away from my insecurities and my troubles
i wish i could grab your arm and bring you here
but you are what i need to get away from
i'm sorry
even though you're the one that should be sorry

the light will never stop trying to come in
maybe it's time you drew the drapes back
and let it
maybe it's time you let yourself become
everything you've dreamed of

being apart from you for so long
only made me realize;
i don't *need* you in order to survive
but, learning to survive with you?
hell on earth

i watched as he picked her up
and i prayed he'd never let her down

all of the photos & letters & memories
i had hidden away in a box under my bed
i found myself looking through it one night
& i didn't feel sad anymore
i'm so happy knowing that we loved each other
the best that we could
sure, it wasn't enough
but we tried & tried and it is truly okay
*-we wanted to take on the world, but couldn't even
make it out of this town-*

through the storms
we always came out stronger together,
even we couldn't weather
what came our way this time
this time it was the universe
telling us we had ran our course
isn't that sad but, also sort of poetic?
the stars, moon, sun,
had to step in to pull us apart from each other
that's how strong, and toxic, we were
-i'll love you always-

you don't inspire me anymore

i don't know how to get back
that happy girl i once was
and that terrifies me
-what happened to that spark i once had? have i
lost it?-

do not let his few fake tears make you forget
the hundreds of real ones you shed
every night, after he left

it's when
the sun is about to set
the birds are making their way home
the leaves are getting a final dance in
the wind runs around to say its final goodbye
that i am thankful i decided to stay alive
to witness beautiful moments like these
-depression lost-

you twisted me around
and painted me in different colors
then decided
i didn't fit your standard of art anymore
*-you wanted me to change
and then got mad when i did-*

all my love for you was drowning in that water
that water in that vase full of flowers that i hated
the flowers were wilting,
even they realized you fed them poison
i only freed myself once
i smashed that vase to the concrete with all my
force
-how did you not know i hate red roses?-

all i wish is for your happiness, he said
so why did you only make me cry? i replied
-silence-

sometimes you have to forget what you feel,
and focus on what you deserve

i carried your name around my neck
i turned into "someone's"
no longer did i embody that freedom i craved
nobody saw me anymore,
all they saw was you
because
i carried your name around my neck

don't call me at night
when you're on your third bottle
you can't even stand any longer so you're leaning
on the ground for comfort,
the empty room keeps laughing at you
and that's when you realize
i was the only one willing
to help you up from the floor
that's when you start scrolling for my name in
hopes of hearing my voice…
but i'm telling you right now, i won't answer
don't call me at night

they screamed at me to shut myself up…
and i listened
-how i broke my own heart-

he will never have another girl like you
you will never have another guy like him
-a blessing & a curse-

i don't want to push it and push you away,
please stay
-messages i sent to a boy that didn't deserve me-

we would spend the whole day
sticking knives in each other's backs
we would spend the whole night
cleaning the wounds
only to wake up and do it all again
-we're toxic, baby-

"i want a break"

    "people don't come back after breaks"

"i know"

    -how you broke my heart with 6 words-

i watched as she clutched her pillow at 2:30am
and screamed out for him
she was drowning herself in tears by 4:50am
her hands were shaking and
it was as if the sky was crying with her
i was begging the sunrise to come & comfort her
because my words were not enough anymore

these boys have not been kind to you, my love
i would say, *"it's not your fault, he's just an idiot"*
but you're still the one
that welcomes back that idiot
with your arms wide open
& your heart ready for more rounds
-he's not going to change and you can't make him-

i'm sorry i said one thing and did another
-i did that a lot-

how do i wish you the best
when you wish me the worst?
-i want to be the bigger person but it hurts-

you lost everybody because of him,
and in the end…
you don't have him either

the boy i once loved, no longer exists
it's as if an empty ghost came
and took his place
he's changed so much
i don't think he even remembers who he used to be

today we got asked to write about Love.
it's not a name, yet it was capitalized in the prompt.
want me to describe Love as a person?
Love is a bitch. Love was first Lust
& decided to try to get in it for the long haul,
who the hell knows why? Not I.
maybe Lust wanted something Lust couldn't have
& had to camouflage itself as Love.
why would a pure thing such as Love
want to ruin its name?
was it I that made Love do those things?
am I really to blame?
for being foolish, naive, and completely vulnerable
to a precious Love.
I'm not stupid for giving in to Love,
I'm not stupid for believing in Love
when I should've listened to Insight
and Common Sense,
I'm not stupid for trying to tag Hope into this
Helpless filled battle.
that's where the issue was;
at the end it was a battle.
a battle of Purity and Dominance.
a battle of Content and Greed.
a battle of Love and Lust.
a battle of You and Me.

i want you here to define what you believe love is
if you told me you loved me,
why'd you ruin me?
is that love to you?
ruining somebody and
expecting them to wait for you?
it wasn't like this at one point
what changed your view on love?
-please don't say i ruined it for you-

you placed a certain hatred in my heart
for some time i couldn't quite figure out
how to diminish it
until i woke up one morning after a storm
and finally understood what it meant to love myself
i haven't known hatred since
-and i hope you haven't, either-

hi.
you've made it to the end, thank you.
thank you thank you thank you.
Alhamdullilah for everything.
i'm so grateful to put my words out there for you.
you have my memories in your hands now.
this is the most nerve-wracking thing i've done.
i literally want to puke writing this but it's okay.
this is also the most vulnerable i've ever been.
writing has saved me in many ways &
the unwavering support from my parents & friends
means the world to me and i wouldn't have had the
confidence to do this without them. thank you.
mom, dad, bekir, amra, azra, merim, lily, bryant,
thank you.
-it always gets better-

Adela Muhic

Made in the USA
Monee, IL
14 June 2020